IT'S MY BODY

Nancy Dickmann

Published by Brown Bear Books Ltd
4877 N. Circulo Bujia
Tucson, AZ 85718
USA

and

G14, Regent Studios
1 Thane Villas
London N7 7PH
UK

© 2025 Brown Bear Books Ltd

ISBN 978-1-83572-007-3 (ALB)
ISBN 978-1-83572-013-4 (paperback)
ISBN 978-1-83572-019-6 (ebook)

All rights reserved. No part of this book may be reproduced, stored in a retrieval system, or transmitted, in any form or by any means, electronic, mechanical, photocopying, recording, or otherwise, without the prior written permission of the copyright holder.

Library of Congress Cataloging-in-Publication Data available on request

Designer: Trudi Webb
Design Manager: Keith Davis
Children's Publisher: Anne O'Daly
Picture Manager: Sophie Mortimer

Picture Credits
Cover: Shutterstock: Blueatro r, Tatila l, Tenstudio and Shutterstock Vector Stock Library.
Interior: Shutterstock: Amahace 21, Blueastro 8, BRO vector 4, 19, bus109 14, Colorfuel Studio 9, Flash Vector 17, Good Studio 5, 6, 13, lemono 10, mentalmind 16, Naaya_Art 18, PetiteARTist 15, Sabel Skaya 7, Mascha Tace 12, Visual Generation 20, Zuperia 11.

t=top, b=bottom, l=left, r=right, c=center.

All other artwork, Brown Bear Books and Shutterstock Vector Stock Library.

Brown Bear Books has made every attempt to contact the copyright holder.
If you have any information about omissions, please contact: licensing@brownbearbooks.co.uk

Manufactured in the United States of America
CPSIA compliance information: Batch#AG/5662

Websites
The website addresses in this book were valid at the time of going to press. However, it is possible that contents or addresses may change following publication of this book. No responsibility for any such changes can be accepted by the author or the publisher. Readers should be supervised when they access the Internet.

Contents

Awesome Bodies 4

Differently Abled 6

Love Your Body 8

Feeling Good 10

Taking Control 12

Personal Boundaries 14

Staying Safe 16

Changing Bodies 18

Take Care of Yourself 20

Your Turn! 22

Find Out More 22

Glossary 23

Index 24

Awesome Bodies

People's bodies come in all shapes and sizes.

There is one thing that belongs to you all your life. It's your body! Your body is pretty amazing. It grows and changes. It repairs itself, such as when you scrape your knee. Your brain is part of your body. It lets you feel emotions. You can laugh and cry.

As you get older, your body will grow. It will change in other ways, too.

People can be different sizes. They can have different colored skin, hair, and eyes.

All Kinds of Bodies

Some people are tall, and others are short. Some people have brown hair, while others are blonde. What color are your eyes? Do you have freckles? Is your hair straight or curly? No one on Earth looks quite the same as you. We're all different, and that's okay!

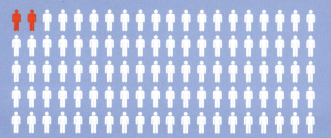

Black is the most common hair color. Red is the rarest. Only **1 or 2 in 100** people have red hair.

Differently Abled

Some people's bodies look or work a little differently. This is called disability.

Many disabled people have body parts that are missing or not working. A person with a disability might use a wheelchair. They might have a dog to help them get around. Disabled people can still do most things. They work, play sports, and create art!

Some people are born disabled. Others become disabled because of injury or illness.

Invisible Disabilities

You can't always tell if a person is disabled by looking at them. Some people can't hear or see well. Others can't hear or see at all. Some people have trouble learning or dealing with people. People with disabilities deserve respect and kindness, just like everyone does.

Tech Help
Disabled people often use tech in their daily lives. Hearing aids help them hear. Prosthetic arms or legs replace missing limbs.

A disability doesn't stop someone from playing and having fun.

Love Your Body

Your body image is how you feel about your body.

Do you ever worry about how others see you? These worries can make you think your body isn't good enough. It's easy to compare yourself to images online. But all bodies are different! There is no need to hide yours. You shouldn't feel ashamed.

Who are you on the inside?
That's what's really important.

Pictures you see online are often edited. Digital tricks make them look "perfect."

Stay Positive

You are more than just the way you look! Focus on the amazing things your body can do. Try not to compare your body to others. Instead, spend time with people who make you feel good. They don't judge you on how you look. They value you for who you are.

How can you improve your body image?

A. look at pictures of actors and models

B. make a list of the things your body can do

C. criticize others about their appearance

Feeling Good

Do you feel positive about who you are? That's self-esteem!

Good self-esteem means seeing the good things about yourself. You feel proud of who you are. You believe in yourself. You know you're a good person. But it doesn't mean bragging about being the best. Self-esteem is confidence that you feel on the inside.

Doing kind things for others can boost your self-esteem.

Try setting goals for yourself. Making progress will help you feel good.

Feeling Low?

It's not always easy to like who you are. But it's important to be kind to yourself. Make a list of things you do well. It might surprise you! Always try your best. Remember that it's okay if you don't win every time. And don't be afraid to ask for help!

Children have a sense of self-esteem by about **5 years old**. They can feel good or bad about themselves.

Taking Control

Does it feel like you have control over your life?

Imagine you're on a ship at sea. It doesn't have sails or a motor. It just drifts with the wind and currents. Does your life ever feel like this? Now imagine that you could steer the ship. You can take it wherever you want. You'd be in control. This is called agency.

With agency, you can steer your life the way you want to go.

Kids need adult carers to help make big decisions. But are there some you can make yourself?

Which of these is an example of agency?

A. choosing the new color for your bedroom walls

B. deciding what to write a report about

C. picking the games to play at your birthday party

D. all of the above

Making Choices

Agency means being able to make choices that affect your world. It might be as simple as choosing what to wear. It might be helping to plan meals. Having agency helps you learn to make good decisions. You don't feel stuck. You feel like you can change things for the better.

Personal Boundaries

Is there a fence around your school? This is a kind of boundary.

Some boundaries are invisible. They're your personal boundaries. They are the point at which you say "no." Someone who grabs things from you is not respecting your boundaries. Neither is someone who tries to get you to do something wrong.

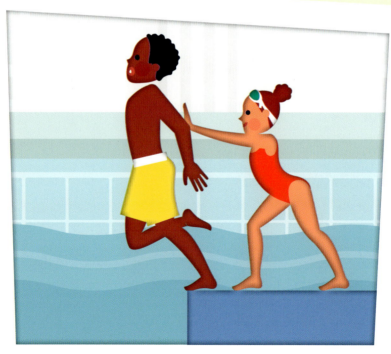

If someone hits or pushes you, they are not respecting your boundaries.

Saying No

If you don't want to do something, you can say no. That's not always easy, especially with friends or family. But a grown-up can show you how. Remember that you are in charge of your own body! Other people have boundaries, too. You need to respect them.

What to Say
"No thanks" is a polite way to say no. If someone does something you don't like, say "Please stop." Or how about "I don't like that"?

Everyone's boundaries are different. Some people like hugging. Others don't.

Staying Safe

Sometimes adults treat kids in a way that they shouldn't.

Hurting a child is called abuse. It might be yelling or threats. It might be slapping or kicking. Someone might touch a child inappropriately. They might even ask a child to touch them. All these things are kinds of abuse. They are always wrong.

Underwear or a swimsuit cover parts of your body. These are your private parts.

If talking about it is scary, you could write a letter. Then give it to a trusted adult.

What to Do

Always tell a grown-up if this happens to you. You could tell a parent, teacher, or school nurse. You might feel scared or ashamed. But remember, abuse is never your fault. Your trusted grown-up will know what to do. They will keep you safe.

Changing Bodies

Your body has already changed a lot. It will change even more!

Think about what you looked like as a baby. What's different now? You're taller, with longer arms and legs. You have a mouthful of teeth. You might even have some adult teeth already! Your hair is longer and thicker. Your muscles are stronger.

Babies can't take care of themselves. As you grow, you can do more things.

Hair often turns gray or white as adults get older.

Which of these body changes will happen as you grow up?

A. baby teeth replaced with adult teeth

B. the fingernails stop growing

C. sense of hearing gets better

What's Ahead?

Your body will keep changing as you grow up. You'll get even taller and stronger. Your body's shape will change. You'll grow hair in new places, such as under your arms. Your brain changes, too. It gets better at solving problems and making decisions.

Take Care of Yourself

Your body does a lot for you. Your job is to take care of it!

One of the best ways to help your body is to eat a healthy diet. Choose foods from all the food groups. Load up on vegetables and fruit. Avoid sugary foods. You should also get plenty of exercise. Staying active makes your body stronger. It helps it work better!

Staying active can be fun! Anything that gets you moving helps your body.

Clean and Rested

Keeping your body clean will help you feel good. Take regular baths or showers. Wash your hands to kill germs. Keep your teeth healthy by brushing twice a day. And don't forget about sleep! A good night's sleep will keep your body working well.

Protection

You can protect your body from harm. Wearing a bike helmet protects your head. Using sunscreen protects your skin.

Sleep helps your body rest and recharge. It gets you ready for the next day.

Your Turn!

You can take charge of your own body!
Here are some ideas.

1. Make a plan for staying active. Choose what to do and set goals. Try to get friends and family involved, too! Reaching your goals will help you feel good about yourself.
2. Find photos that show you as a baby, a toddler, and growing up. Put them in order and look to see what's changed. How do you think you'll change as you continue to grow? Draw a picture to show what you might look like as an adult.

Find Out More

Books

Olson, Elsie. *Be Strong!: A Hero's Guide to Being Resilient (Be Your Best You!)*. Minneapolis, Minn.: Super Sandcastle, 2020.

Richardson, Ashley. *Your Body Belongs to You (Take Care of Yourself)*. Mankato, Minn.: Capstone Publishing, 2021.

Woolley, Katie. *Resting and Sleeping (My Healthy Life)*. New York: Rosen Publishing, 2024

Websites

www.healthforkids.co.uk/staying-healthy/

kidshealth.org/en/kids/self-esteem.html

wonderopolis.org/wonder/whats-best-about-your-body

Glossary

abuse causing someone harm, such as by yelling, hitting them, or touching their private parts

agency the idea that you have the power to make choices that affect your world

body image how you feel about your own body, particularly the way it looks

disability a condition that affects how a person lives their life, due to part of their body not working as normal

emotions feelings such as happiness, anger, fear, or sadness

food groups the categories that foods can be placed in, such as meat, grains, or vegetables

germs a name we use for various kinds of tiny living things that cause illness

hearing aid a small device worn in the ear that helps someone hear better

personal boundaries the limits and rules we set for ourselves and our relationships with others

private parts the parts of a body that are covered by a swimsuit or underwear

prosthetic an artificial body part designed to replace a natural one

self-esteem a feeling of confidence about who you are

Index

A
abuse 16, 17
agency 12, 13
asking for help 11, 17

B
babies 18
bodies 4, 5, 6, 7, 8, 9, 15, 16, 18, 19, 20, 21
body image 8, 9
boundaries 14, 15
brain 4, 19

C
changing bodies 4, 18, 19

D
disability 6, 7

E
emotions 4
exercise 20

F
feeling good 9, 10

G
growing 4, 19

H
hair 5, 19
having fun 7, 20
healthy diet 20
hearing 7

K
Keeping clean 21
kindness 7, 10, 11

M
making choices 13, 19

R
respect 7

S
saying no 14, 15
self-esteem 10, 11
setting goals 11
sleep 21

T
worries 8

Answers to questions

page 9: B (pictures online are often unrealistic and made to look good, while criticizing someone else's appearance is unkind and won't make you feel better about your own)

page 13: D (even small choices like the options here can help you feel more confident about making decisions and improving your life)

page 19: A (although your 20 baby teeth will eventually be replaced with 32 adult teeth, your fingernails never stop growing, and hearing often gets worse after the age of about 50)